Table of Contents

Anger and Abuse	1
Best Friends	2
Changes and Solutions	3
Expressions of Sexy	4
Integrity	5
The Mind's Eye	
The Bully	6
Secrets	7
Loyalty	
Faith	
Waves of Emotion	8
Solitude	9
The Rock	
Life's Expectations	10
Fantasy or Reality	11
The Influence of Words	12
In a Numbers World	13
Drops of Water	14
Pride	
Depression	15
Stitches in Time	16
Intelligence Earned	17
Easy Access	18
Gossip	19
Damage Control	20
Lost Touch	21
Fairytale of Ordinary Life	22
Mom and Sons	23

Anger and Abuse

Teardrops fallen from the faucet into the sink
Watch while it showers your weakened heart
Audacious as you can be to accuse,
Yet, no bravery in your soul,
You were born to protect, you run when challenged
No Attrition in your eyes or heart
Captivating you victim, you attempt a fierce
Vicious bash to the face,
Startling that victim until the fidelity is no more,
Faith wary, hope scorned.
Only tears as they moisten my cheeks.
Anger runs through my body as you try to contend
Through the haze of tears, words that have no meaning.
Trying to make you understand, another critical blow,
With words, you condemn my very being.
Exaggeration as you try to blame.
No way to defend myself from your words with no meaning

Best Friends

Enjoy my innocence
Time will endure
Even though loyalty's
Put strain on us
Hold on to hope
Faith in the uncommitted
So we may grow together,
Courage to carry on
Embrace when we are needed
Sentiment in becoming one
A relationship worth having
Trust in one another
Without reservation or concern
Impressions with the heart
Talking and understanding
Listening and communicating
No anger in words to regret
Beauty in honesty and contribution
Between two best friends
Appreciating each other
An affection to nurture

Changes and Solutions

When the world doesn't seem to fair
All hopes seem to fail, go to a place of peace
Let all worries go, relax…..
The same problems will be there tomorrow
So why let it ruin your day, look ahead,
Tomorrow is another day, new hope will come to light
Focus on the future
Problems have a way of working themselves out
Gloom has no room for faith, believe in new things
Solutions will come in time, don't waste your day in dark shadows
Embrace what is in front of you
Tomorrow will be a good day for changes
Positive wisdom on a piece of paper

Expressions, of Sexy

To the girls who think that dressing Sexy is right, think again!
Sexy is what you cannot see
The essence of an action
Reaction, a thought, an image
Irresistible temptation
What the mind wants to believe
Women think they need to look the part
Not so, quintessence, concentration
It's beauty that can't be seen
A man's attention is caught up in vision
Hallucination of a mental picture
Prediction of what might be, a women's innocence
The likeness of the idea, a view of what could be
If you think you're sexy, it depends on who is looking.

Integrity

Honesty in being true to yourself
Truthfulness in the mind of what is good
Reliability in completing what is asked
The uprightness of what is accomplished
As long as we live by these few words
We will live out our lives with Integrity.

The Minds Eye

What the eye sees.
 My minds eye, I vision
What the eyes will see
Far and wide, flowers, trees

The Bully

One who preys on your vulnerability
Pushes people around, takes away your pride
Because you want to fit in, do what is asked
Jealous because you have something unique,
What the tyrant doesn't have, so the aggressor pushes and belittles

Criticizes, so it hurts, can't turn the tide, no one will listen
It continues, you pay money so the thug will stop
Now it's gone viral, you trust the intimidator betrays
Everyone believes false truth, looks of disgust
It was never your fault, just a jealous person
Wanting to destroy your innocence

The torment of hidden truth, instead of making an ally
Choose to destroy the opposition
Like a game they have to win.
No one asked to be bullied, they see the exposed
Hone in one the weakness, knowing they will concur
Somehow they seek the ultra-sensitive part that makes them strong

Because they have the power to crush your dreams
Today it's your hair, walk, the make-up, style of clothes
Anything to embarrass, that will give them power,
Think again you tormentor, I am better than that
Will not stoop down to your level, I see what you don't have
My life will go on, and I'll get through this rock in the road
Leave me alone, I have nothing for you.

Secrets (Haiku)

Mysteries yet to unfold
Confidences shared
Riddles with amazing revelation

Loyalty (Haiku)

Trustworthiness earned devotion
Consistency in dependability
Allegiance in friendship

Faith (Haiku)

Belief in commitment
Dedication in confidence
Assurance in your trust.

Waves of Emotions

Melancholy is an existence of realities that make us miserable
As I walk along the beach where waves are crashing in the distance by the rocks
An unhappy moment that passes through the silhouettes
I watch the angriness in the swells as they splash and roll back
Time that heals all wounds, but recollections, always there to remember
Watching the collision of water verses surges of swells
Take you back to the time when things were not highly regarded
Hiding the truth, so innocent... I'd recognize what you tried to conceal from me
 Always knew, felt it in the defiance of your approach
Like a waves inconsistency, the brash manner in your opinions
They lacked responsibility, no maturity,
Leading me to and fro, like the movement in flowing breaks
Someone else was at fault, never yours, ripples of water on the seashore
I would cry myself to sleep no more, watch the surges of emotion
Showering me with spray, as they crash against the rocks

Solitude

Privacy is when you can sit back
Take the surrounding that you are in, simply enjoy the view
Being at peace with yourself, a way of coping
This world is ever changing, you can't modify or alter,
Nothing we can do about that
Sit back take it in and be patient
In the end it will all work out.

The Rock

I am a rock, hard and stern
Camouflaged with armor to protect my soul
Unsympathetic to nature and her mood swings
Uncompromising to the hiker who trips and sits on me
Unyielding to the kid who throws me
Easygoing to a fault, serious about my place
When threatened, I stand my ground
I can be smooth or rough on the outside
Or shine with crystal, opal or gold
Life, grows around me, I maintain my stamina
On a mountainside or ocean floor
I've stood the test of time
I am a rock, I will stand forever

Life's Expectations

Time passes, days linger
Memories are left behind
Twilight glistens as we pass
Stars surround us with rays of glitter
Shine to escort us throughout the way
Lives we touch daily, fears we put aside
Teardrops shed along the way, with circumstances
Enlighten our dilemma
We travel through time that will mend all wounds
Heal the pain and start anew
The road of life we travel
Starts over at another turn
Through doors yet unopened
With difficulty and emotions that give us preparation
Educate us with experience

Fantasy or Reality

Bitter sweet words out of your lips
Remind me of unpleasant sorrow
For love is crucial, when shared by two
Split between one another, unrehearsed
Spontaneously, amplified by sensitivity
Trusting your lovers perceptions
Incorporating independence, respect
Igniting a fire, exploding with need
Becoming one so delicately, embracing me close, encircled
Bask in the glow of sentiments and vibrations
Cuddle each other to a soft squeeze
Reinforced by moment in time
Where we were mutual in an individual instant

The Influence of Words

The power of words, impact you
Feel joy or guilt, laughter in a story
Beliefs taught through the ages
Words have domination
They are the application of intelligence
Teach, judge, apply to well being
Verses, memorized, lesson taught
All would be lost, if not for vocabularies
Song lyrics tell of love lost
Poems of inspiration, stories that dispute battles of freedom
Speeches of promises to come
Just confrontations that promote potential
Tales of untruths, feelings hurt
Terms of expressions that can't be taken back
Anger metaphors that invent coinage
A moment to live through without regret
Should have been discussed without drama
Exaggerations in a flash of annoyance
Simple words we use everyday
Never realizing the impact they have
Choose your vocabulary carefully
Make a difference in your language
We all listen, but don't understand
Someday we will be on the same page

In a Numbers World

Your birthdate and your name have a significant number
Math is done in figures of sequences for solving problems
Just use the sums, and the information amounts to a total
Modern math has shortcuts, they teach you in school
Scientist us them to calculate, manipulate the digits
Statistics of facts, integrate into quantities
Algebra, geometry, trigonometry, and calculus
To a Genius that's no challenge to a beautiful mind
Addition, Subtraction, Multiplication, and Division
Different ways to come to sums; Romans used numerals
Chinese us an Abacus when counting, Accountants use them to balance books
Computer programmers use them in their paths to clarify the keys
Everyone uses numbers in everyday life
Play games of Sudoku, Karuko, Rummy, Spades, Dominos
They all teach you to use numbers that make your mind remember

Drops of Water

Through the drops I see a stream
Water washing all the leaves away
Cleansing the soil they lie on the land
New growth will begin
Rain water rushing to a place unknown
Bathing and rinsing it all away
Fresh water meets the ocean
Fusing to become one
Earth has a way of renewing itself
Make everything fresh and new
So should our lifecycle

Pride

A man's pride shall bring him low
But, he is that is of lowly spirit
Shall attain honor
Let not your heart envy sinners
To be in fear of the Lord all the day
For surely there is a future
Your hope shall not be cut off
The lust of a man is his shame
A poor man is better than a liar…

Depression

Mirrors on the wall
Reflections of you
That's all that's left
My heart has stopped crying
All that's left is a dim memory of you

Shadows cast silhouettes on the wall
Sometimes it feels like you're near
But, it's only my heart beating
As I listen to the music

The nights are so cold
The warmth in my body has gone
All I Feel is empty
Darkness has brought my soul, Silence

Someday the emptiness will be gone
Someday the shadows will be lost
The nights will no longer be cold
But the memory will be planted in my heart forever.

Stitches of Time

Learned to stitch when she was six
Grandma by her side a sampler was born
Teaching new stitches they shared time
Going through and learning more stitches
Children came she'd sew, by hand and machine
Stitches of time

With each stitch she'd sew with love
To share with those held close to her heart
Sitting on a chair now making Quilts
Stitching each stitch with love
For when this Quilt is done
It will be given to a grandchild to keep them warm
Stitches of time

Show much love that will warm the heart
Teaching a grandchild the stitches learned
Tired she falls asleep knowing that what was left behind
Her memories long remembered to pass through generations
Stitches of time

Intelligence Earned

Learning is a state of mind
From the time when babies
Acquire the knowledge to walk and talk
Without parents' watchful eye,
The next step must be mastered:
Reading, writing, arithmetic
Schools and teachers are the next mentors.
We become educated, getting the message through.
Tests develop into a way of verifying what has been crammed in our heads
Proving we comprehend and understand the lessons
Moving up the ladder of grades
Spending life with your nose in a book
Adolescence sets in and weakens our abilities,
Maturing and less absorbed in book work;
So much more to memorize and experience,
Getting the hang of reality and the world
Graduating and college to be attend
Facing new challenges, determined to succeed
Admiration for the lessons still left to unearth,
Improving the mind and building a background.

Easy Access

Interesting stories the mind can predict
Imagination has a way of stretching the predicament
Twisting and changing what the truth once was
There's a reason for each man to be
Making the challenge high
Changing the score, accomplishing more
Feeding the mind new data
Distorting and modifying the schedule of tasks
Taking on new configurations to become a competitor
Defeating the monster of high intelligence
Stopping the movement so he is cornered
Conquering the bad guy, ah, the next level
Suddenly gasping, my provider has pulled the plug!

Gossip

So the saying goes
"There's two sides to every story "
Don't believe everything you hear
Point your finger
Look around at the one who's talking
No one bothers to ask
The one being talked about
Yet everyone points the finger
Shame on you for accepting untruths
Told out of spite
Because you were left holding the bag
Open your eyes find out the accuracy of the lie
Or are you the one pointing the finger
Without knowing how much actually
Is what you heard

Damage Control

The human spirit is very fragile
The saying goes: "You're such a strong woman "
Not so, you're on the outside looking in
Mask the real person who hides from
The reality of criticism
Offend people with the truth you speak
Maybe they don't want to hear, so they cry
Talk about you behind your back
As if the rumor will not support the truth
To haunt you, because of what is said
Yet you may not defend
Damage control cannot be done
Friendship lost because your wisdom
Is much too exceptional for the human spirit,
Maybe to precocious for you

Lost Touch

Places to go when one has lost touch
Hidden from the outside world
No one can see, yet the mind searches
Through the haze of lost identity
Shadows that linger in the dark
Destiny of faint, belief
Recognizing those closest to you
Yet not recollect,
Fear of what has become
A stare, unclear
Doubt, no answers
Just of what is missing
No words to describe the fear
Tears of loved ones misplaced
Yet, through the blur,
Something, familiar
A scent of perfume
A contact, well remembered
For a second, then all is vanished
A minute, well spent, a touch lost

Fairytale of Ordinary Life

He searched through modern technology
Contacted her, she answered
They planned to meet on an island
Turn back the clock to calculate, what the future held
Once in awhile, we step back
Go to places in the storage locker of the mind
Old lovers caught up in a whirlwind romance
Walk beaches with bold sunsets of orange, yellow, and red
For a brief moment they stare into each other's eyes
Alone on a beach, they ignited that glimmer that was eternity
Letting the beauty of the heartening, atmosphere
Take flight and escape the battle of nonexistence
Twisted rapid tumultuous emotions
Swiftly taken by amazement, holding hands, sharing
Divided by reality, or a dream, affecting sentiment, soul mates
That wonderful, flawless, unspoiled man
That charms her images at night
Takes a journey from the ordinary to the fairytale
Of wonderful, steadfast, dependability
The constant, devotion of being loved

Mom and Sons

As I watch them sleep, they look so peaceful
Who would have thought that these two bundles of joy
Would breathe as much life into one's heart
Every morning to wake with hugs and kisses
Lunches to be made and off to school
Asthma attacks, scraped knees, cut and scratches
Both come crying to Mom
I never realized the needs two little boys have
Homework, girls, bikes and sports
Never a dull moment, so much time and love to give
I wonder if they'll outgrow that need for Mom

www.ingramcontent.com/pod-product-compliance
Lightning Source LLC
Chambersburg PA
CBHW030046230526
45472CB00005B/1708